Table of Contents

Rourke Educational Media

A Division of Carson Dellosa Education

rourkeeducationalmedia.com

Can you find these words?

dusk

feast

moon

pray

We Celebrate Ramadan!

Ramadan fills the ninth month of the Islamic year.

Let's watch for the new **moon.**

Ramadan begins.

Let's fast.

Adults do not eat from dawn until **dusk**.

Let's give.

Share with the needy.

Let's pray.

Muslims think about their beliefs.

Let's have a **feast**!

A party to end Ramadan lasts three days.

Did you find these words?

Adults do not eat from dawn until **dusk**.

Let's have a **feast**.

Let's watch for the new **moon**.

Let's **pray.**

Photo Glossary

dusk (dusk): The time of day when the sun sets, just before dark.

feast (feest): A large, fancy meal shared with family and friends.

moon (moon): The natural satellite that revolves around Earth about once each month.

pray (pray): To give thanks, ask for help or forgiveness, or focus on beliefs.

Index

About the Author

Lisa Jackson is a writer from Columbus, Ohio. She likes to ride her bike and collect pennies. Her favorite holiday is the one that is coming up next!

www.rourkeeducationalmedia.com

PHOTO CREDITS: Cover: ©By arapix; Pg2, 12, 14, 15 ©happy_lark; Pg 2, 10, 14, 15 ©PRADEEP87; Pg 2, 4, 14, 15 ©Ig0rZh; Pg 2, 6, 14, 15 ©leolintang; Pg 3 ©wsantina; Pg 8 ©By Kertu

Edited by: Keli Sipperley
Cover and interior design by: Kathy Walsh

Library of Congress PCN Data
Ramadan / Lisa Jackson
(Holidays Around the World)
ISBN 978-1-73160-578-8 (hard cover)(alk. paper)
ISBN 978-1-73160-453-8 (soft cover)
ISBN 978-1-73160-627-3 (e-Book)
ISBN 978-1-73160-690-7 (ePub)
Library of Congress Control Number: 2018967335

Printed in the United States of America,
North Mankato, Minnesota